Awaken Memories

Awaken Memories

Poems by Ruth Friedberg

ISBN 978-1-893054-52-3

Cover: Watercolor painting by Sam Friedberg, *Ruth on the Steps*, 1970. All artwork in the book by Sam Friedberg.

Published by Word Design Press

CONTENTS

LINGERING (Late Poems)

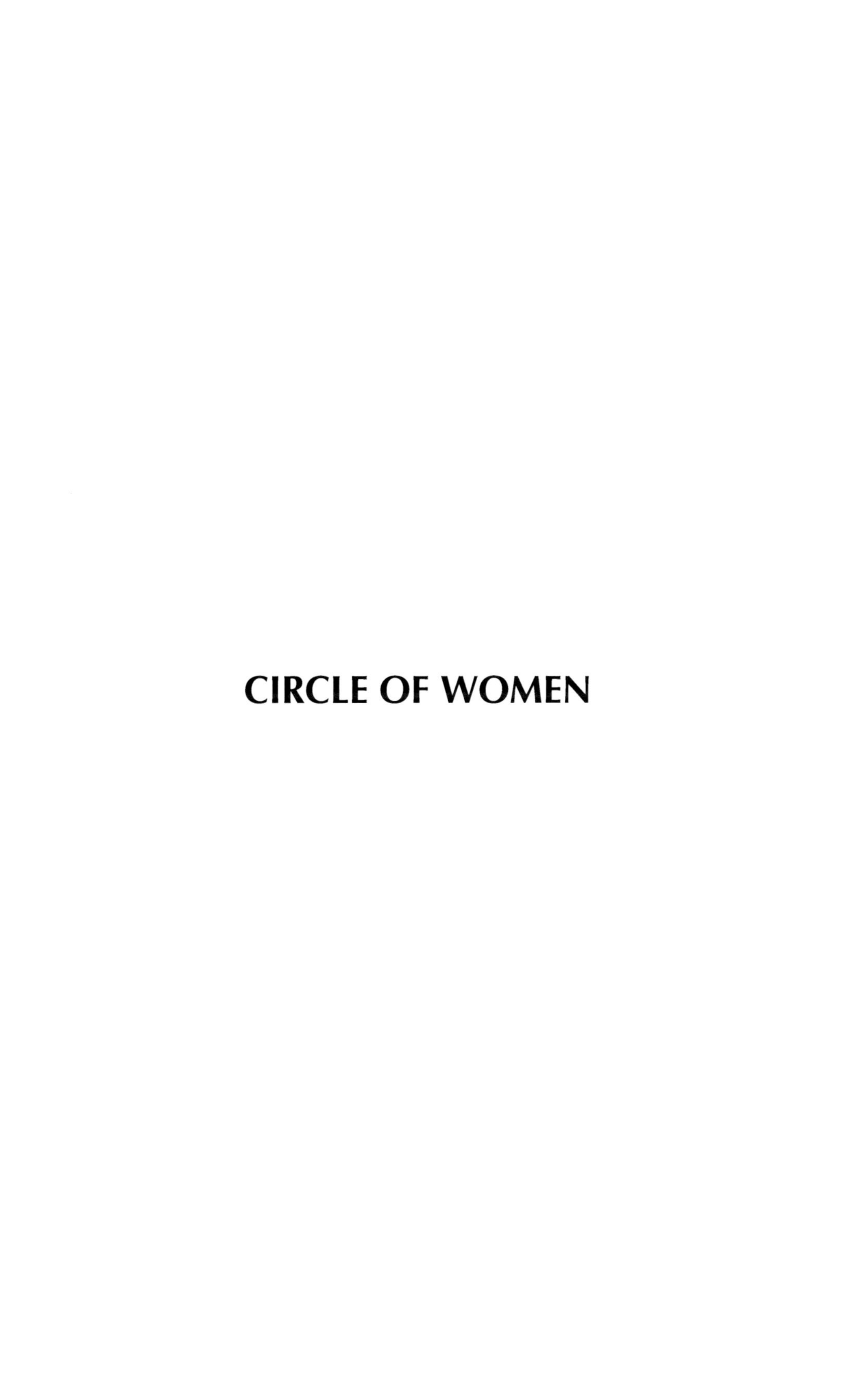

CIRCLE OF WOMEN

Doris

This passing
Cannot be mourned.
Only approval
For the end of pain,
For the watchers' release,
For the soul's flight.
But the unshed tears
Swell in the throat
And gather behind the eyes.
Not for her—
Radiant spirit soaring—
But for us,
Banished from the warmth
Of her presence.

Charlotte

She stepped lightly
Into his life
With careless grace
And beauty unaware—
Opened his heart,
Revealed his love,
Then quietly
Slipped away.

Gert

Ever since she left
At any hour
Of the day or night
She speaks
Inside my head,
Calling my name—
That only—
With husky insistence.
Then,
Replacing the heavenly phone,
She turns
To her appointed tasks:
Painting the angels' wings
In azure,
Jade, and amethyst,
Interviewing God on Eternity,
And checking His credentials.

Ruth

I am Ruth
Maker of songs
Daughter of moon
Sister of starshine.
I sing of lovers
I sing of mourners
I sing of the dawn bird
Fiercely trilling
And of the night wind's
Gentle sorrows.
All that is
Between the heavens
Weaves and sighs
In the song
And my heart floods
And rests.

Poem by Ruth C. Friedberg

Music by Lawrence Weiner

III. Ruth

Rather slow and gentle

dawn bird Fierce - ly trill - ing And of the
night wind's Gen - tle sor - rows.
All that is Be -
tween the heav - ens
Weaves and sighs weaves and sighs In the
song And my heart Floods and rests.
Broaden
sub. p
cresc.

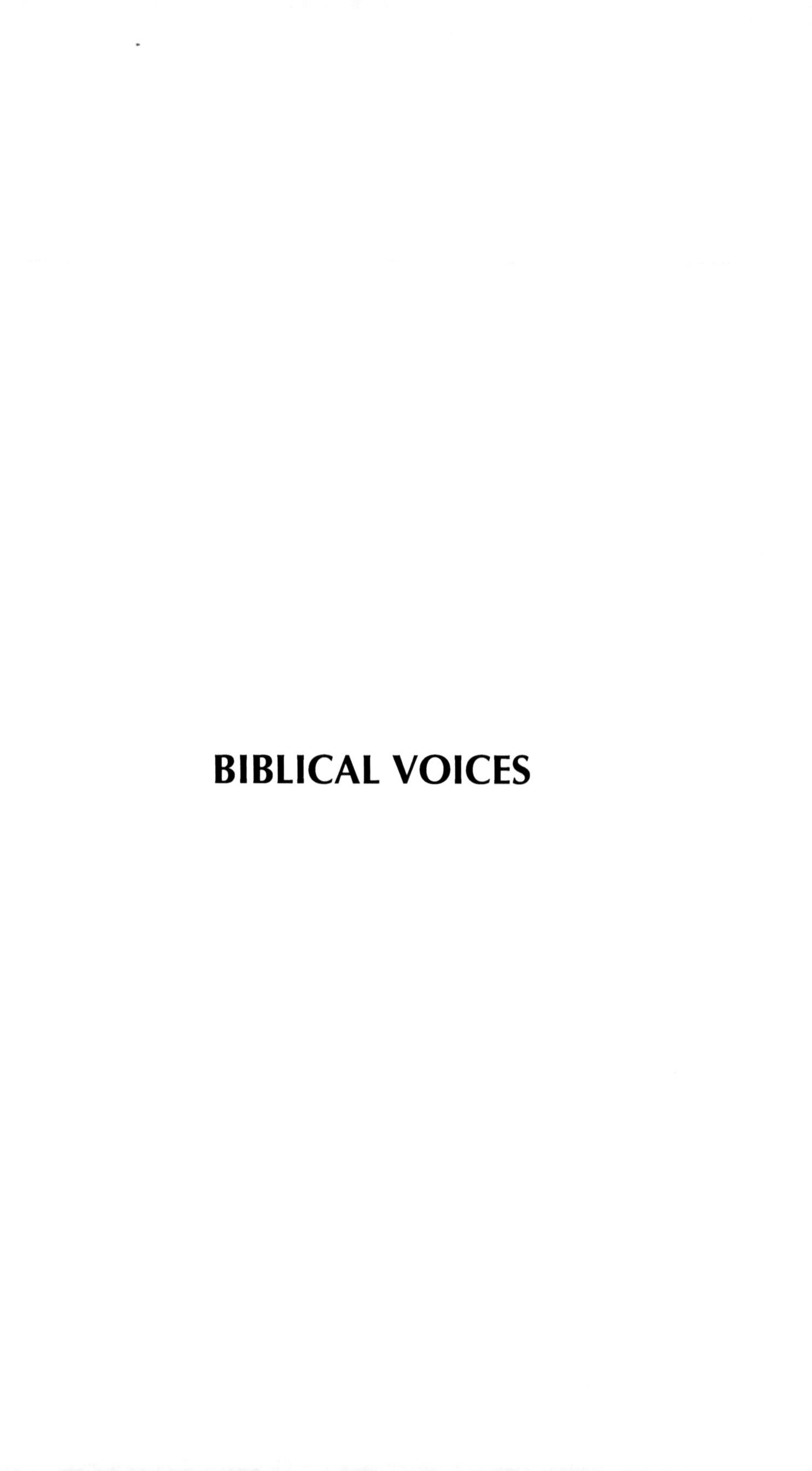

BIBLICAL VOICES

Adam's Version

What did she want?
I love her but I've never understood.

There, the trees were tall and shady,
The ripe fruit fell at our feet,
The breezes touched our bodies gently
As we lay caressing.

Now the sun burns us,
The barren earth leaves us hungry,
And the children come
Through her agony.

What did she want
That I could not give her?
I will never understand.

Sarah, Dreaming

Night after night
the children come.

They swell in my womb.
I carry them
in my arms.
They grow
before my eyes
and speak words
of sweet wisdom.
I sleep in joy
and wake to emptiness.

But sometimes
there is blood
in the dream
and the child
cries to me
stretching out
his little arms.
I scream
for Abraham
but he is silent
and his God
moves toward me
in a dark shadow.

Friedberg

The Sisters Speak

Leah

Ashes and dust around me
A dark sun in a dark sky
For never will he turn to me
In the fire of his longing.
My sons grow tall
But the light in his eyes
Is for her only.

Did you ask me, God,
To choose my blessings?
Did you ask me
How many sons
I would give up
For the beauty
That haunts a man
Forever?

Rachel

My sorrow is deep
It chokes my life
It follows me
Into his bed
And I lie in his arms
A beloved, barren woman.
Never does he reproach me
But Leah's sons
Grow in his image
While I give him
No new life.

Did you ask me, God,
How much beauty
I would trade
For my place in the birthing tent?
All of it, God,
And life itself
If that is Your bargain.

Friedberg
2000

Dinah

My father speaks to God.
Does he mention
The unloved daughter
Of an unloved mother
For whom he cannot weep?

My mother prays to the Goddesses.
Did she forget my name
When on her knees
She begged for
Blessing and protection?

My brothers talk of honor,
Theirs, not mine.
And they write their words
In the blood
Of a man who cherished me.

I speak of nothing,
Listening to the wind
Blow round my tent
As the sun sets red
Over Shechem.

TEFILLOT L'SHALOM

TEFILLOT L'SHALOM

I

Open me, God,
To Your presence.
Enfold me
In the blessing
Of peace.
Let me breathe in
The shining stillness
And breathe out
My gift of silence
As the world's turning
Becomes its rest.

II

God—
You who write
History
In the human heart—
Make us responsible,
Make us compassionate,
Make us powerful
In our loving,
And bring us
Toward peace.

III

God of Light
And Darkness,
Help me
To find my
Wholeness.
Let me embrace
The shadows
'Til they turn
Radiant
As the sun.

IV

Let my I-ness
Join with Yours
In unending
Praise
Of Creation.

Let Your peace
Be my peace
And let us dwell
Together
At the singing
Heart
Of the world.

V

I have become
No-self.
I am absorbed
Into the peace
Of God.
I am
No longer aware
Of the boundaries
Of my skin
Against the air.
I merge
Into the Sound
Of God

And into the
Light
Which fills
And creates
Worlds
Without end.

Invocation

Come,
Angels of Rest,
Surround my bed
With the soft
Rustling
Of your wings.

Come,
Angels of Light,
Let your radiance
Fill my dreams
With meadows of gold
And hills
Of amethyst.

Come,
Angels of Peace,
Shield my sleep
From the dark
Messengers of the night
And hold me
Safely
In your gentle
Rocking.

Angel Flight

I dreamed of angels
And I rose
With them
Into the welcoming
Air.
High above hills
And houses,
Beyond the blue,
Shimmering earth,
Climbing
Into the bright
Darkness
Of all beginnings.

Surrounding me
In joyful flight,
They murmured softly
In a long-forgotten
Tongue,
Holding me gently
Amid their tender
Rustling.

Stranger to fear,
Wrapped in love,
Lost to Time,
I flew on 'til
Morning light.

They kissed me,
Then,
And I awoke,
Mourning the lost Presence,
Trembling with certainty,
Swept by joy.

FROM THE NURSING HOME

From the Nursing Home

My beloved father died in his bed at fifty-five,
His generous heart vulnerable to attack
In a world before the by-pass.

I was twenty-four years old, my son barely three months.

I never got over it......

After twenty years of widowhood,
My mother languished in the hospital
Following an inept hip repair.

Courting death there, as an escape from pain and fear,
She was restored to six more years of life

By an elegant nursing home
Where I became a frequent visitor......

Miriam

My mother was a lady.
I never called her *Mom*.
There was always care
And a perfectly tended house
But no warm and enveloping lap,
No ready shoulder to cry on,
Not even, in time, for small grandchildren
Whose presence threatened assault
On her ordered spaces.

Now, in the nursing home,
She is never Miriam.
The nurses call her Mrs. Crane
As they arrange
Her lacy bed-jackets.
Her room is large,
Furnished with many of her treasures,
And looks out on
Trees, grass, and ducklings.
She will not leave her domain,
So I visit from far away,
And am particularly summoned
At holiday time
When I present
Small gifts to the staff
Who hold her comfort
And her life
In their hands.

Too many breaking bones
Have placed her
In an unrelenting wheelchair.
She sits,
Watches families,
And interprets her past.
Are you close to your husband?

She asks me.
Yes, I reply. Were you and Dad close?
Shades of regret cross her face.
I could only be
As my parents raised me, she says simply,
Offering me the rich gift
Of her hard-won insight.

One month later, appears
The merciful stroke
That answers
A devoted physician's prayers
For her release.
Now she has
No questions.
Only the pressure of a single hand,
A small, gentle smile,
And soft words of love
For all of us,
Even those
Who have arrived
Almost too late.

....

Several years after my mother's death
I agreed to return to still familiar territory.

This time I would come as a musician,
Surrounded, as I believed, by the performer's insulation
Against excessive empathy......

Alma

The group congregates
In the rec room,
Carolers around the piano,
Myself seated at the keyboard.
In the assembled wheelchairs
The residents listen,
Hum along, doze.

After the session
We visit with our audience.
I am drawn to a beautiful face,
Framed in silver hair,
What is your name? I ask.
Alma, she answers,
And as we talk
Her soft voice stirs chords
Of memory and longing.
I'll come back
And visit you, I say.
She smiles gently.
That would be nice.

Months pass, filled with
Too busy and Maybe tomorrow.
Finally, a rainy afternoon-—
I arrive at the reception desk.
I'm looking for Alma,
Room 204, I think.
Alma?— her shocked surprise
Telling me what will follow.
She passed away—
Two weeks ago!
Were you a friend of hers?
No, I say, Yes!
The breath gone out of me,
Awash in sorrow

And guilty shame,
Unable to remember
What had been more important.

……………………

Time passes.
Friends sicken,
Some move quickly
Into death.
Others linger,
Diminished,
But still cherished……

Alice

She was tall and straight
With the voice
Of an aging angel.
Married at fifty,
She had left behind
The singer and teacher
She was in Chicago,
Joining her husband
In my city
To begin again.

I help her all I can
But it is never the same for her,
A long crawl back up the ladder,
Searching out students
And audiences,
Nurturing
An uncomprehending husband.
At last the struggle ends
In a sidewalk seizure
After our final concert.

The tumor in her head
Grows rapidly:
Swallowing effort,
Swallowing regret.
When I visit
After the Mayo Clinic
And the surgery,
She is in and out of sleep.
But we talk briefly
Of a new therapy.
It’s amazing, she says.
Sharks do not get cancer
And their cartilage heals!
Here: you must

Read about it.
I borrow the book
To share her hope.

Next time I come
The nurse shakes her head.
She sleeps all the time now.
I sit for a long time by the bed,
Saying goodbye.
Later, miles away in my car
I remember that
I forgot to return the book.

Gerard

Performer, composer.
Musician extraordinaire,
Lover of food, laughter,
Conversation,
Beloved of students
And colleagues,
Friend of my many years,
His streaming life
Now circumscribed
By the explosion
In his brain.

Halfway down
The anonymous hall
I find the number
Of his room.
Answering my knock,
He shuffles slowly
To the door,
Placing the walker,
Dragging the leg
He can no longer
Command.

The small piano in his room
Lies silent.
The right hand
Has lost its movement
And the left,
Its will.
I have him read with me
A child's book
Of great composers.
The words come haltingly
And he cannot relate them
To each other.

Time passes slowly,
Filled with loss.
As I rise to leave,
I remind him of my name
Which he will never again
Recall unaided.

But the radio
Is playing
And his face
Lights up.
That's Cesar Franck,
He says joyfully.
Testifying
To all the music
Still living
In his head,
Undestroyed.

....

By now, the Nursing Home
Is a well-known entity.
I answer the call
To visit strangers,
Only to find
How quickly they become
Endangered friends......

Ada

She is ninety-four
And very small
In the bed.
Do you rcmcmbcr me? I say.
Of course I do,
The mind and tongue still sharp.
Do you read much?
Never—can't see to.
And talking books?
No patience—and my hearing's bad.
Do you visit with the others?
Not very sociable, I guess,
She reads my mind,
But I'm afraid of death.
After that
We sit in silence
As the day wanes.

Bernie

Sound asleep, he sits
Straight up in the chair
By the window.
His checked vest
Is carefully buttoned,
Cap at a winning angle.
If I pass him by
He will miss the visit.
Hello, Bernie, I say,
Very close to his failing ears.
His eyes fly open.
How are you today? I begin.
Now the struggle to return,
To affirm remaining life,
After a hundred and two charming years
The spark still kindling.
So good to see you, darling—what do you call
That color you're wearing?
Once again, I am seduced.
I listen to his familiar stories,
Remind him of my name
And the members of my family.
When it is time to leave,
He rises with his cane
And escorts me down the hall.
Give my regards to the doctor, he says,
With a rakish tip of his cap,
As his once and dancing feet
Move slowly to ancient memories.

Bernice

The room is richly furnished,
Heavy curtains drawn.
She cannot see the light
Or its absence.
How nice you look, I say.
What a pretty dress!
Which one is it? she asks.
I can't quite make it out.
Images flow
On an enormous TV screen.
Shall I turn up the sound, Bernice?
No, she says, I'm not really watching.
I show her the cassette player
And tapes I have brought—
She cannot find the "on" button.
But she knows her pictures on the wall,
Each engraved on her inner sight.
This was my house, she says.
I didn't want to leave it,
But they said I had to.
It's beautiful, Bernice, I whisper,
My eyes filling with the tears
She cannot afford to shed.

Raye and Jean

There are nine children
All left motherless by the
Demon flu of 1918.
The orphanage becomes home
For Raye and Jean,
Now a close-knit
Family of two.

Grown to womanhood,
Tall and lovely,
They do not marry.
They work in offices,
Worship on Saturday,
Build a life
For each other.

When I find them
In Room 114
They are still together
At 90 and 92.
Jean is hard to understand
But not for Raye.
She speaks for both,
Offering me chocolates
And thanks
For my little gifts.

Later, I discover that
They are the last
Of the siblings,
A far-away niece
The only living relative.
A lawyer handles our affairs—
He's very nice, says Raye,
Still at home in the world
In her family of two.

On a cold January day,
Raye is taken to the hospital.
She does not return.
Puzzled, Jean lingers briefly,
And follows Raye in April.
They were joined at the hip
Observes the Rabbi
At the second funeral.
And at the heart, I whisper.
A family of two.

SEASONS

Seasons

I. Summer

I lie
Helpless, pinned
To the earth by shimmering
Waves of heat. Above
My vanquished head
A curious
Butterfly
Circles.

II. Autumn

Autumn winds
Moaning in the branches.
I must hide,
Lest winter
Find me.

III. Winter

Bare,
Ice-laden trees
Hang low over deserted paths.
In the frozen ground,
The daffodils
Tremble.

IV. Spring

Spring
In the Valley,
A gentle wind coaxes
The orange blossoms.
Beneath your hands
I, too,
Awaken.

Seasons

Poem by Ruth C. Friedberg

I. Summer

Music by William Gokelman

Roman Dawn

I waken
Into the morning light
As clouds of swallows
Wheel and cry
Beyond my window.
Soft air tumbles
My gauzy curtains
And the street sounds
Begin to gather.

On my balcony
The flower boxes
Slip into color—
Wild fantasies
Of cabbage roses
Flaunting
Their improbable heads,
And geraniums, brilliant
Against the earthen tiles.

Across the city,
The sun splashes
In the silent
Trevi fountain.
On the Via Veneto,
In the elegant cafes,
Flagging tourists sip
Caffelatte,
Gathering strength
For another day
Of wonders.

The Coliseum shudders
In its ancient bones,
The Spanish steps
Prepare their assignations,

And in the Borghese gardens,
Lovers linger
In the coolness.

Spoleto, Early June

The city rises quietly
From a stretch of grassy meadow,
Spiraling upward
Toward the Umbrian heavens.

Narrow medieval streets wind
Past nestling boutiques
And market squares
Breaking open to the sun.

The ancient amphitheater
Lies still,
The stones awaiting
The crowds and music.

San Eufemia stands
With rounded arches
Bathed in pale
Twelfth-century light,
As nearby, the Gothic Duomo
Shelters Filippo Lippi.

At the very top,
Unearthly beauty
In all directions.
A Roman aqueduct
Become a bridge
To a fairy-tale palazzo,
The Italian hills
Stretching into the distant haze,
And everywhere, fields of poppies
Thrusting their crimson warmth
Amid the tender green.

Florence

In the Ufizzi palace
The staircase winds
And stretches steeply
To the treasures above.
Panting, triumphant,
I attain the galleries.
And there, beyond Leonardo,
Past Botticelli,
And through the open window
Lies Firenze bella,
Clothed in all her glories
Of russet, cream, and gold,
Shining in an emerging sun
And preening for our delight.

From a Mountain Lake

I

The breeze
Across the lake
Brings the scent
Of fresh-cut
Grass.
Memories awaken.

II

Dried branches
Lie across my path
They tremble
As I approach
With heavy step.

III

Ducks in the water
Fight over my crumbs.
One flies to me
But will not
Eat
From my hand.

IV

Leaves on the hillside
Touched with red.
Death
Stalks the smiling face
Of summer.

Landlocked

The sea bore me
nourished
my childhood
always at night
falling asleep
to the rhythm
of waves
crashing
on the shore

In a beautiful
inland college
nestled
in the hills
I am sleepless
perplexed
by the silence
finally knowing
I have lost
my sea

Summer

The unlikely
resplendent rains
have greened
my garden
grass shooting
skyward
trees bending under
erupting branches

But the crape myrtle
does not bloom
the esperanza will not
unfold into golden
even the stalwart plumbago
withholds
the color has gone
with the artist
and I remain
in a monochromatic
World

Autumn

Is there any
Poetry left?
Did I spend it all
In middle-aged
Adventures?
Is there nothing saved
For the quiet years
When the blood
Runs slower
And the gathered
Fruits of wisdom
Rest
On a dusty shelf?

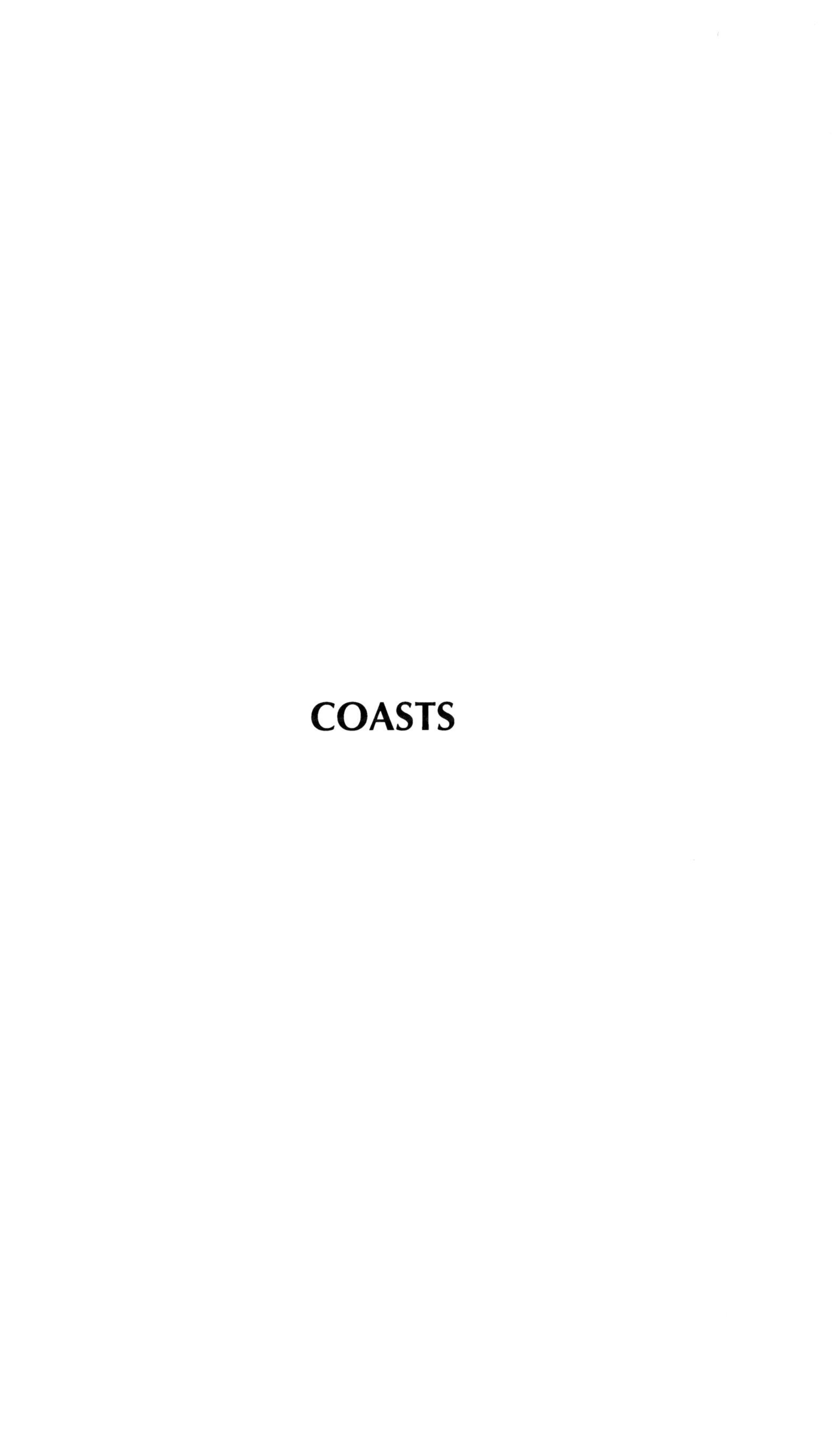

COASTS

Walking The Edge

My feet invade
The languid borders of a wave
As sand crabs scuttle
Toward shelter
From the intruder.
A pallid sun
Confers a grudging benediction
On crowds of worshipers.
Beyond them lies the Boardwalk,
Spreading its carpet of planks
Before the elegant, aging hotels.
Turning my head, I see
The gray-green stretch of limitless water,
Broken by white foam
In an unending dance.
Bright sails fattened in the wind
Punctuate the horizon,
As a veering gull
Dives suddenly toward its prey.

Atlantic City, NJ
1940

I am twelve years old.
My father's house is four stories tall
And filled with the warmth of his presence.
It is an ordered, glowing house
Which my mother tends with gentle, fluttering anxiety.
A safe place
To be a child, with sheltering
Porches and the steady bedtime roar
Of friendly, reassuring breakers.
But the monster in the dark
Has already been encountered.

His name is Death, and he has taken
A grandmother, moaning on the floor above through a year of
nights
And a school friend, suddenly,
Lost to the disease that is
The terror of children.

I am twelve years old
And begin to understand
That only the frenzy of Love
Can dispel Death's abiding menace.
I am learning to giggle at boys
And I rehearse in poetry and novels
My vision of the future.

Always, in all seasons, there has been
The beach and the stretching water
Forming my boundaries, whispering
Of outward passage.
And now I am twelve years old,
Walking the edge,
As the sand, pulled by a strengthening tide,
Begins to shift.

A Coast at War

Two miles
Beyond the breakers
The great fish lie in wait.
The ships go down, their oil
Bleeding
Slowly onto the sand.
The tall hotels
Have lost their glittering ladies.
Now they are filled with boys
Who drill on the beaches,
Preparing their deaths.

One hotel is a hospital.
Its corridors, stripped of heavy carpeting,
Invite the wheelchairs.
On the boardwalk, now barely lit,
Uneasy nighttime strollers
Strain to see each other's faces.

Atlantic City, NJ
1943

I am fifteen.
The house is cold and empty.
Fuel is scarce,
And my father has gone to war.
The sky is gray,
And a leaden sea
Shrinks
To the shaping of our fear.
Gulls circle
Like menacing vultures
Over the anguished writhings
Of possibility.

And floating
Just above the horizon
The bright face of the future turns
To a gleaming skull.

Two

A deserted beach,
As yet undiscovered
By fashion.
Rocks lying warm
In the mid-summer afternoon.
Beyond the dunes,
A scattering of cottages
Bordered with zinnias curving
In the sea-winds.
We sit on the sand,
Close, yet separate.
I turn my head toward him,
Toward the dark, serious face
That broods against the sun.
His khaki pants and sober shirt
Indulge my frivolous bathing suit.
He does not swim, and warns me
"Don't go too far out."

I am nineteen
And no longer alone
In my ocean.
Archly, I venture beyond the breakers,
Savoring his gaze,
Shivering in the rising promise
Of vulnerability and delight.

Brigantine Island, NJ
1947

Loss

I push the carriage
Down the boardwalk.
My son stirs
And our eyes meet.
Joy hardly blossoms,
Only to wither
In the now familiar
Rush of pain.
My father is dead
And this child of my body
Will not remember his smile.
He closed his eyes
On the first of spring
And was buried
In its grieving rains.
It is a fierce spring
And I lean
Against the wind, knowing
That with the blooming of his roses
The worst is still to come.

Atlantic City, NJ
April 1953

Turning South

Soft, seductive, mysterious,
The Old South envelops us,
Where confused ghosts
Of rice and indigo planters
Hover
Above the Parris Island recruits
At drill, under a steaming,
Relentless sun.

Leaving Beaufort,
We skirt the tidal channels
Flanked by tall, shady houses,
Then cross the bridge
Between shrimp boats
Clustering at harbor.
I drive my son across
the sea-islands,
Past shanties of the turbaned
"Gullah" blacks
And solitary oaks weighted
With streaming moss.

Hunting Island State Park, SC
Spring 1955

At last, the Atlantic,
Lying broad and free.
Its shallow, indolent waves
Lapping a sultry beach
With its fringe of bright palmettos.
We inch our toes
Toward the water,
To find them warmly bathed.

And now my son begins
His occupations,
A small, sturdy three-year-old
Moving purposefully
From sand-castles

To tube-floating
To marine biological explorations.
He is absorbed, responsible,
Self-contained.

How long, then, shall I mourn
The others
That will not grow in my body?
On this strange, exotic coast
Of burning sand and
Caressing waters,
I am again, as forever, Between—
Floating, here, in a shallow pool
Filled with the heady blossoms
Of forgetfulness,
Silent as in a dream
And motionless,
Waiting for floodtide.

Rebirth

Before
The bridge was built
It could be a long wait
For the ferry
At Albemarle.
Five hours' drive
To the Outer Banks
From our lush Piedmont enclave
Of ivy and bell towers.

But then, what glories!
In incredible joining
Of northern turbulence
And southern flow.
Nags Head first-—
Fierce waves
Crashing
On blistering sands
And seaside restaurants
Oozing tempting smells
Of succulent bluefish
Nestled in "lace bread."

Then down to Hatteras
Along a narrow road
Whose drifts of sand
Whisper
Of wind and storm
While peaceful fishermen
Pull opulent piles
Of flounder
From the fickle surf.

Finally, Ocracoke-—
Dreamlike visions
Of wild horses

Outer Banks, NC
June 1957

Trampling the sea grass
And an insubstantial village
Of islanders
Frozen in time
With angular accents that recall
Elizabeth the First.

The surf pounds,
The horses whinny,
My Self uncurls
From its fetal sleep
And rises,
Glistening
Like a newborn.
Here, here will be the place
Of the miracles.
For this,
Known unknown,
Is the country of the heart.

Friend

This is a different sea-—
Landlocked, of drawn boundaries.
Constricted, it strains against its bonds,
Throwing its spray higher,
Gathering the sun to itself
In glittering bursts.

The dunes are smaller, too,
But rise in stubborn, crystalline thrust
Toward the stark, blue challenge.
Bathers are set
Like jewels of many colors
Against the sand and sea,
And a noontime brilliance
Defies the turning earth.

Lake Michigan
August 1962

I am with my friend,
Dearer to me than lovers,
Formed of my rib
And lodged in the brain's joining.
Four years down the street
In our university town-—
Four years of daily commerce
That fed my bones-—
Then separation, letters,
And yearly trips
Of a few days' meeting
To talk into the dawn
While the children sleep.

Now we are come to the Lake
With her small daughters
To forget the sadness
That has torn her life,
And to release the floods of joy
That surge between us.

But our time is running out
And the joy turns brittle,
Hard-edged, like the sunlight.

I, too, am in bondage like this inland sea,
Locked into the space between us
And the years we cannot share.
Shouting and splashing, I race
Wildly into the water,
Straining to hold the moment,
But the shards cut my feet
And a cold wind
Blows from the dunes
Before the waves take me.

Pilgrimage I

Knokke, Belgium
July 1963

Long before
He became my husband,
He had described
The beauty of this place.
"An overrated childhood memory,"
I had thought,
Still worshipping
At the shrine of the familiar
New Jersey strand.

Here, at last,
In the Old World,
The youthful chauvinist
Is shamed.
Knokke is dazzling,
With brilliant flowerbeds
Enfolding every boardinghouse,
An elegant road of tile
Stretching along the beach,
And the proud, scrubbed cleanliness
Of the North.

Looking to the right,
Out beyond the breakers
Is a distant point of land,
Faint in the bluish haze.
"That's Holland," he says,
Still
With an echo
Of his far-off
Boyish wonder.

French Riviera
July 1963

Ville-Franche
May have been a mistake.
Our quaint, inexpensive "pension"
Simmers at ninety-five degrees

And we toss at midnight,
Dreaming of fans and ice-cubes.
My son, now ten,
Has wistful visions
Of a lost Little League season,
While I repent
Whatever sin of inappropriate need
Has driven me across the Atlantic.

Mornings are better.
We climb into our rented "bug"
And, windows open
To the sultry breeze,
Skirt the blue-green Mediterranean:
Past the gleaming hotels of Nice
And on to the magic coves of Cap Ferrat;
Turning east to Monte Carlo
Or up into the painters' hills
Where Van Gogh broods
Over every field of wildflowers
And gnarled country face.

Best of all, the wild,
Heart-thudding ride
Along the Grand Corniche.
High above the towns
I sense
The curving flow
Of this ancient sea,
Mother of all the civilizations
That have bred and formed me.
The car lurches, I cry out
In fearful joy,
Knowing that this pilgrimage
Is accomplished.

PHAR

Flight

Silent and terror-stricken,
I assume
My usual hunch by the window.
Now,
Cleared by the tower,
My husband banks the plane
Eastward to the ocean.
We turn south,
And it begins.

Gasping in delight,
I forget
The nibbling headache
And queasy inner lurches.
No giant transport this
With a tiny peephole
At five miles up,
But a magic carpet
Flying at eight thousand feet,
With a wrap-around,
God's-eye view
Of a transfigured coast.

South Atlantic Coast
November 1966

Almost forty years
By the ocean's edge,
Never dreaming what this would be—
The border of waves and sand
Become a continent,
And I, the heavenly cartographer,
Tracing
The thrust of the Outer Banks,
Approving
The islands of Georgia
Showing gently brown
Through a gleaming sea.

Evening is falling
As the Florida peninsula
Begins to form.
Our destination
Has become the Emerald City,
Flickering
With the thousand lights
Of enchantment.

Landing
Will be the hard part.
Being defined again
By friends,
Remembering
The newly discovered damage
Of our adopted child,
Returning to the snares
Of the earthbound.

For a final moment,
I cherish
The splendor of this suspension
Between sea and sky,
And celebrate
The powerful beauty
Of the Now.
Then the runaway
Rushes up to meet us
And we are caught again
In becoming.

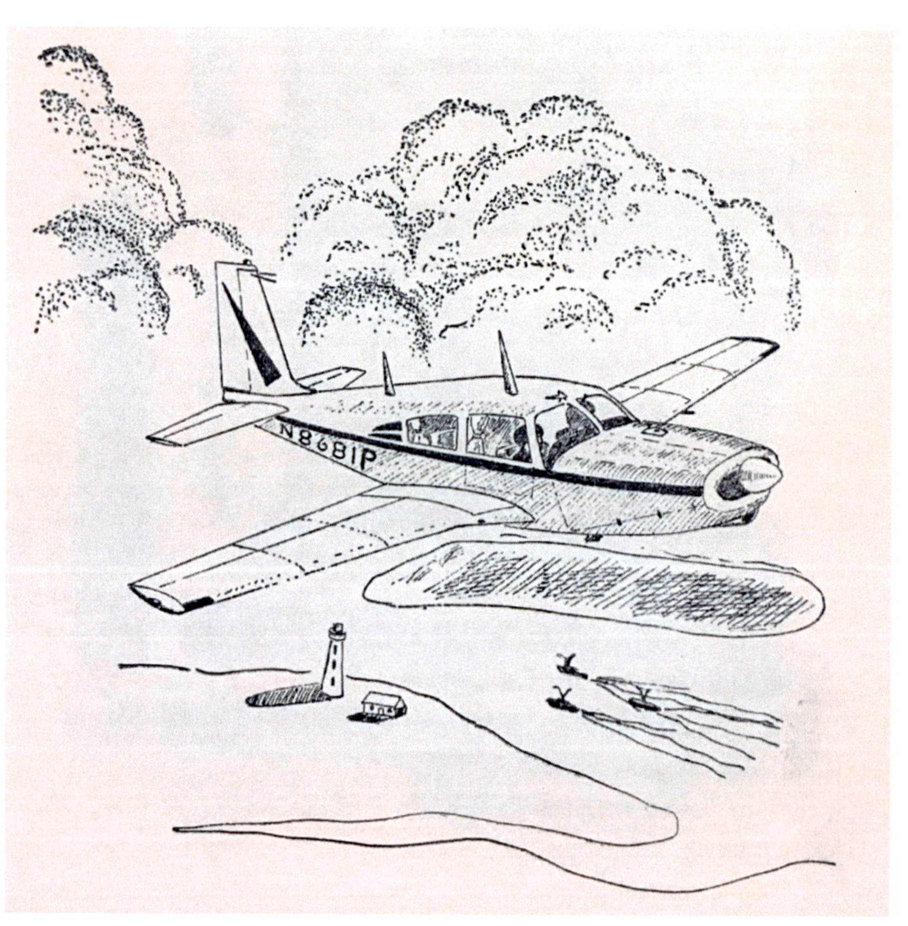
N8681P

Adrift

Beside our balcony,
Tall palms rustle.
White sands,
Edged in jade,
Bloom with umbrellas of thatch.
The sun slants downward,
Its daily fury spent,
And in the softening light
I see
Two bathers
Lost in each other,
As he gently
Combs her hair,
Working damp strands back
From a beloved face.

Luminous against the sky,
They feed my darkness.
Caught
Between an old love
And a new,
I am come again
To this ocean-—
For solace,
For wisdom,
For surcease of tearing,
For obliteration
Of thought and feeling
In the searing days
And dancing nights.
But the couples
Surround us
Honeymooners and lovers
In bright array,
And there is no forgetting.

Nassau
July 1967

On our balcony
At midnight,
I curl into the shadows,
Watching,
As on an impassive, onyx sea,
The moon
Daintily etches
Her silver path.

Madonna and Child

Long, golden hair
Shining in the sunlight,
My small daughter
Weaves between the sandhills
In purposeless,
Desultory motion.
She has no words, and her frequent
Anguished crying
Cannot be comforted.

Tonight,
The lazy swelling of the Gulf
Will not lull her to sleep.
Driven by her brain's firings,
She will roam
Until she drops;
Finding, in the miraculous respite,
A desperate courage
For the new day.

We two are encaged
By this grueling Texas sun—
Caught in each other's Fate,
Thirsting
For release.
But the sand-grasses
Throw only tantalizing
Spikes of shade,
The Gulf affords
The barest cooling,
And the beach-buggies,
Radios blaring,
Explode into view like visitors
From another level
Of the Inferno.

Mustang Island, TX
August 1969

Low Tide

A glassy-eyed fish-head, left
On a whitening skeleton;
Rotting boards,
Whose rusty nails menace
The unwary;
Shells in profusion,
Broken and whole;
And the empty bottles
Of old revelry...
The ebb-tide slowly
Uncovers
The oceanic debris-—
A mirror-image
Of my inner landscape.

Atlantic City, NJ
September 1973

Footsteps falling slowly
Into wet sand,
I assess my wreckage:
Two divorces
In as many years,
A distracted son in college,
An eight-year-old daughter
Recommended for "residential placement,"
Grief beyond tears,
And fear
That rises with the morning sun.

Landward, too,
Is ebb-tide.
The great hotels have faded,
Once-proud facades
Crumbling in neglect.
The Boardwalk
Has been deserted
By the rich and glamorous,
Now jetting to Acapulco

And the Costa del Sol.
In their stead,
The aged pensioners
Shuffle slowly to their places
In the pavilions…

I will join
Your pale assembly.
I will creep back
To my mother's house,
And end my days
Hidden in your midst,
Crouching low
On my bench
Lest Life again discover me.

A stranded sand-shark
Flips hopelessly
Toward water.
The September beach
Stretches
Its grey, lonely length
After the retreating waves.
Cringing against the wind,
I face the sea,
Watching for a sign,
But the tide is relentless,
And it does not turn.

Pilgrimage II

First love, first husband,
Soon to be third,
Joins me
Where the ancient sands
Cover the bones of our people.
Here
At the eastern end
Of this mythic sea,
We are lost in glimmering visions
Of mariners, zealots, and warriors,
Borne in
To these exotic harbors.

At Acre
We lean precariously out
Over the huge stone battlements,
Become crusaders
Watching Saladin's
Inexorable approach.
Climbing the tower,
We view the old city
From Ahmed-el-Jazzar,
Then feast on grilled fish
By the bay
At Abu Christo's.

Haifa lies
In its painful beauty.
Hill after hill
Of domes and gardens,
Just as it beckoned
Half a century ago,
To the ships
Full of hollow-eyed refugees,
Seeking a sanctuary
Too often denied.

Israel
July 1975

For us, a secure haven,
In the welcoming home
Of old friends,
Who display the wonders
Of Mt. Carmel, the Technion,
And Haifa Bay in the settling dusk.

Then down the coast
Through Caesarea,
Lavish pleasure-city
Of the bloody Romans,
Where sea-grasses
Flourish in the arena,
And sands drift carelessly
Against the mighty arches
Of the Imperial aqueduct.

Tel Aviv at last,
In all its bewildering variety-—
We linger
Over luxuriant fruit stands,
Elbow our way
Into crowded buses,
And idle in the sidewalk cafés,
Of the Dizengoff,
Trying vainly to evoke
The sandy desolation
Of an earlier day.

The old port city
Of Jaffa
Draws us to its labyrinth
Of shops and studios and galleries.
In the market, we haggle
Over a jingling
Yemenite necklace,
And a burnished copper pot
To fête our coming home.

At sunset, we dine
High above the turquoise sea-—
Pilgrims awash in history,
Lovers by grace reprieved.

At the Center

In a rainy spring,
The coastal roads
Blaze with wildflowers—
Wave after wave
Of purplish blue,
Salmon-pink, then tender
Whites and yellows,
Spreading into summer
In profligate display.

The goal of our royal journey
Is Rockport, Texas—
A tiny fishing village
Nestled
Against Aransas Bay,
Where visitors' lodgings
Do not tower against the sky,
And the sea-birds
Find quiet shelter.

Rockport, TX
August 1980

Our rooms
Are in a cluster of buildings
Fashioned of creamy stucco,
And topped in red-tiled roofs
That burn against the azure.
Steeped in a lifetime
Of music and words,
I long now
For a brush and pots of paint
To manifest the delight
This color breeds in me.

A palm tree
Leans above the patio.
With scraps of charcoal,
I follow its curve

Onto my drawing pad,
Distracted only
By the wheeling of gulls
And cormorants
Above the fishing pier.

How curious to find
The inner eye
Growing keener
And more enraptured
With the physical world,
As the outer dims
And the Mystery deepens.

The bay is calm—
A yellow sunfish
Drifts slowly in toward shore.
A great blue heron
Poses majestically
On a piling,
And tiny black-eyed susans
Dot the grass
Down to the water.
My edges
Disappear in oneness
And I am whole.

LINGERING (Late Poems)

Surfers

The young gladiators
Come from the sea,
Carrying their boards
Like shields of honor,
Long hair flying,
Bodies lean,
Striding triumphantly
Into the wind
In proven mastery
Over a weedy death.

Retreat at the Coast

I am tired of words, God,
Tired of prayers and incantations,
Tired of proofs, denials,
And evidence,
Of reasons why
And why not.
I will speak to you
In silence
And I will hear
Your answer
In the roaring surf,
In the screech of gulls,
And in the secret rustlings
Of the sea-grass.

Bermuda Honeymoon

We'll take your picture, she says,
If you'll take ours.
Strong, tanned, young legs,
Hair streaming in the sultry breeze,
Eyes bright with expectation.

My husband and I
Sit for our portrait:
A seasoned couple,
Fully clothed against the warrior sun,
Slender but thickening,
And fifty years beyond the wedding day.

Their turn, then,
Arms entwined, but still
A little awkward in their joining.

I long to tell them
Of what will come,
Of the tangled path
That they will travel.

But they are straining
Toward the water,
Careless of the reefs,
And warning fades
Before their certainty.

Have a nice life, I breathe,
And let them go.

For Sam

All those years
Side by side
I seldom wrote
About you.

Our shared life
Was the reality,
Poetry the fantasy,
One step removed
From the actual.

Now you are gone,
Ashes safely tucked
Into the earth,
I write about you
As I mourn,
Sensing a new,
Unwelcome
Reality.

Grief

New grief is
blood-red
drops oozing
from an open wound
deepened
by each day's
waking.

Old grief is
pale
smothering
in scar-tissue
as the wound
widens out
to the shape of
emptiness.

Untitled

every
summer morning
we breakfasted

near the greenery
surrounding
our favorite
porch

lost in conversation
or in being
together

now I am
alone

discovering
the dazzling flights
and piercing songs

of a hundred birds
that have always
shared my space

unseen
unheard

The Letter (a watercolor by Sam Friedberg)

She sits
on a park bench
long skirt
draping her legs
long fingers
guiding the pen
long hair falling
around her face
the artist's brush
delights in her
as almost woman
poised
on the edge
of life

Gloria

her gentle hands
pluck the covers
reach toward a
growing presence
I take her hand
stroke her arm
touch her forehead
then I begin
to sing
an old song
that long ago
brought comfort
to my sister
and now
the miracle
Gloria sings
with me
together our voices
welcome
her embracing death

The Crossing

My father
left the Old Country
on the last ship
bcforc
World War I
A sweet-faced boy
of seventeen
with a head
full of languages
Russian, Polish, Hebrew, Yiddish
crammed into steerage
teeming with crying babies
and sad-eyed mothers.
Left behind
a mother, father,
three siblings
he would never see again
a leap into the unknown
beckoning the brave
with whispered promises
of an unimaginable
New World.

The Way

The Way In
occupies
a lifetime
the path
appearing
only from behind
there is no
Way Out
in extremis
as a gift of grace
we stumble on
the Way Through

Gratitude

The gift of life
Mysterious,
Unappreciated,
All-encompassing.
We spend our days
Seeking,
Always seeking
The chalice
To receive
Our thanks.

Where I Am Now

Waking up
is the hardest part
remembering the losses
praying to an unknown
Father-Mother God
for the strength
to live this day
clear-eyed in the pain
open to old grief
and what is
yet to come.

Made in the USA
Middletown, DE
08 August 2021

45632980R00058